THE LIFE OF THE SPIRIT

The Spiritual Masterpiece from The Founder
of The Science of Thought Review

by

Henry Thomas Hamblin

Originally published in 1925.

TABLE OF CONTENTS

Foreword

Introduction

Chapter 1 - Initiation

Chapter 2 - Initiation (continued)

Chapter 3 - The Quest

Chapter 4 - The Inner Life I

Chapter 5 - The Inner Life II

Chapter 6 - The Inner Life III

Chapter 7 - The Inner Life IV

Chapter 8 - The Inner Life V

Chapter 9 - Tests

Chapter 10 - Love, The Magic Key

Chapter 11 - How to Meet Life's Difficulties and Perplexities

Chapter 12 - Serving Others

Chapter 13 - Life Without Strain I

Chapter 14 - Life Without Strain II

Chapter 15 - Life Without Strain III

Chapter 16 - The Way of Life I

Chapter 17 - The Way of Life II

Chapter 18 - The Way of Life III

Chapter 19 - The Law of Sacrifice

FOREWORD

INSTEAD of writing a Foreword to this book, I should rather just give thanks that such a great Message is going forth. It is a Message from the heart of the Writer inspired by the living spirit of God.

I have just finished reading it and it has left me with a strong sense of its uplifting Spiritual Power. It is a clarion call to those who really seek the deeper depths, the higher heights, and to enjoy that holy mystical sense of the Presence in such a degree that the whole Life becomes a shrine of worship, until the full Glory of Union is attained.

It has been clearly and faithfully shown that this is no easy path. In this fact of striving lies our whole salvation, because it is God that worketh in us to will and to do of His good pleasure. "Quit ye like men, be strong." This is a call to the noblest within us. Who really wants anything he has not earned?

One knows well enough that Mr. Hamblin speaks the truth when he says: "To those who are in earnest, whose whole desire is fixed upon God, who will not falter . . . these are the ones who go forward, nothing can stay them, for there is no power in heaven or hell that can stop a soul aflame with the desire to find the Kingdom and to see God."

In this Quest we have the Great Adventure open before us with Life as the Initiator, at every step shedding the old consciousness with its illusions—we launch out into the deeps of God and fear not.

St. Teresa says "Alone God sufficeth," and this is absolutely true, for do we not find that all we seek is only to be found in union with the Divine?

All the Mystics down the ages, all the modern mystics tell the same story.

Dwell deep, go within, seek with all your heart, soul, mind and strength and you will not be disappointed. Strong, sure and silent is That Something which declares

Itself to the true seeker. It is this Sun of the soul which colours all the ordinary happenings of Life with a golden glory, changing the grey to gold and bringing into every crisis Light and Wisdom, "Rest after weariness," "Rapture of bliss."

The way Home, as faithfully shown in this little book, may be through experiences which baffle and bewilder, but the Goal is certain.

There is no church large enough to contain this Holy Splendour, there is no creed possible to this sublime understanding. Only Love can understand love and only the God-like can attain to this God consciousness filling all space and yet spaceless. We are all children of the Most High, made in His image and likeness.

Mr. Hamblin says: "This gospel is so simple and yet so difficult." "Only to love, this is all." We are here to give and not to get. To love, to serve, dropping self every moment of the day, so living that others may feel our love, our sympathy, our understanding, and the first door into the Kingdom is opened unto us. Let us give all we have and all we are, this is our sacrifice, our joyful offering to Life.

Well! those who do this cannot write in words the Love which is theirs.

In this little book the many difficulties are met and dealt with in such a way that no one needing help can fail to receive it and gather fresh inspiration from the deep Wells of Truth. They shall walk and not faint in a strength which is unfailing and close at hand.

To some, Christ, so long forgotten, arises from the depths of being with the gracious words, "lovest thou Me?" "I have loved thee with an everlasting Love." "Feed my sheep" — Help others.

In these days of vague speculation and extraordinary cults, we turn with quiet peace to the unfailing strongholds of the Eternal Strength, to the all-sustaining Life of God and His Christ, the sweet, pure, all-pervading Spirit. We know that this Exhaustless Treasure has been available since the foundations of the world and will go on to the end of the ages, for each, and all. Above the changing creeds and many voices Thou remainest, and we are one with Thee.

To this holy Union we turn with longing Desire—it is the end of the Quest; every moment we delay, or move on, towards this wondrous Deification. No one can hinder us but ourselves.

Once fairly started the pilgrim learns that every rebuff is a challenge. Go forward and may the "Vision Splendid" fire the imagination and fill the Soul with positivity, for greater is He that is within than all that is without.

Mr. Hamblin has through much experience attained to this deeper knowledge of the Infinite Love and a rare insight into the Soul's deepest needs.

How good it is to listen again to the sublime words: "Learn of Me for I am meek and lowly." We cannot change the heart by any amount of thinking, but, if we have made the sacrifice the offering of our whole being to the Christ, the thoughts of the heart (which is the Place of Wisdom) flood the mind with purity and strength.

It is at this juncture we join hands with those who are striving to mould the mind into deeper channels for the Supreme Mind to dominate and reveal its hidden treasure, but Christ is ever and always the Door. "Thou hast set eternity in their heart." This is the true immortality and not the life physical, although, when we identify ourselves with the Transcendent Life, our whole being, mind, body, and estate, becomes regenerated by the redeeming power of the Christ nature within.

As this book clearly shows, and speaks with no uncertain voice, all our past steps, as full of limitation as they were, each was valuable and necessary in its order—initiations into wider reaches of Life.

Let us look forward with glowing hearts to the holy consummation, the ineffable joy of Union. This is the Apex of Being, and with our hearts and minds set in this direction we shall be led on from strength to strength, from glory to glory, until

"That which is Perfect is come."

— ALICE MORTLEY, Writer of Christ in You.

INTRODUCTION

THIS little work attempts to deal only with inner religion. In the Spirit we can all become one, although on the surface we may not be able to agree at all. The Kingdom of the Spirit is eternal and unchanging. Theology and doctrine change from age to age, but the inner Spiritual Reality is the same always. Now, as in olden time, we can make contact with this inner world or Kingdom and find God, and in Him be satisfied. Scientific discoveries threaten to overwhelm Christianity from time to time, but they make no difference to the Inner Kingdom. When Science or the Higher Criticism has demolished everything, apparently, the mystic still contemplates the Supreme, and walks with his Lord. Nothing is changed really.

Everything essential is just the same. It is only the non-essentials that have been shuffled about somewhat.

Quite recently there has been a great controversy about Darwinianism. A school teacher in America was arraigned because he taught Evolution. Most educated people in this country accept evolution as a matter of course, just as they accept the law of gravitation. Because of this some think that Christianity is exploded.

But nothing is altered in reality. It does not matter, even if it is the fashion to believe in evolution, for we can retire into the Secret Place of the Most High just the same.

The earth is still the same, now that people believe it to be a globe, as it was when people thought the world was flat. The earth is not altered—it is only beliefs that change.

The exterior part of a religion does not matter much—although it is about this that people quarrel so bitterly—it is its inner meaning and experiences that are of importance. The end and object of religion is Divine Union, and if another soul attains to this blissful state by a different road from that which is the only one that can be used by us, let us be glad and praise God, instead of wasting our time explaining to him that he is wrong and our way the only one. Let us all be broad-minded. Our Lord said, when speaking from the super-conscious, wherein He realized that He was consciously indwelling the advanced souls in every nation and religion: "Other sheep I have which are not of this fold." Let us be glad that this is so, and rejoice in that the Truth can be found in so many different ways.

Strange though it may seem to many, some people are afraid of what is going to become of them when Divine Union takes place. They are afraid that they will lose their personality or individuality. They argue that if they get back to the Father like a drop of water returning to the Ocean, they will be swallowed up and lose consciousness, so to speak. Nothing of the sort happens, of course, the consciousness is not lost — it expands. But this is a great mystery and little can be said about it, but the following, taken from the writings of Dr. Rufus Jones, may prove helpful to some:

"There need be involved no loss of personality, no abandonment of selfhood. The self is not merged into a nameless absolute. Personality remains, but it is now a Personality conscious of its divine environment, conscious that its life is God's Life—a Personality that chooses to will the divine Will and that is conscious of its two sides or surfaces of expression. It all feels, then, as if there is around one a Conscious Ocean, an Ocean of Consciousness with conscious inlets opening out of it—one of which inlets constitutes yourself. The inlet on its shore side may have it, defined shape and margin, but on its seaward side it may open to the ocean and feel the influx of its tides and currents. The tides of that measureless expanse may sweep in to stir the shallows of the inlet. The inlet is in the ocean and the ocean is in the inlet."

May this little book help many pilgrims who are "in the Way" to a deeper realization of God's presence and a more intimate fellowship with their Lord.

H. T. H.

Chapter 1

INITIATION

NOT OCCULT, BUT SPIRITUAL THROUGH DAILY EXPERIENCE

LET it be said at once that the writer does not claim to possess any knowledge of Occult Initiation. What he does know, however, is that life itself is the great Initiator, and that all of us who have set out upon the Path are daily being tested and tried and prepared for higher service. Actually, life consists solely of a series of experiences, and it depends entirely upon how we deal with these experiences as to whether we make any progress along the Path or not.

It is the writer's experience that it is not necessary to practise anything of an occult nature. Some people think that they must wait for some great psychic or spiritual experiences, during which they shall leave their body and go through a Mystic Initiation in which they are tested in various ways. This may be necessary for some, but the writer knows by experience that life itself furnishes a series of tests and experiences which provide all the initiation that some of us apparently need.

"Not everyone that saith unto me Lord, Lord, shall enter into the Kingdom of Heaven." It is one thing to leave all and follow the Gleam, and quite another thing to prove ourselves worthy of our high calling. Those who set out upon the great spiritual adventure must prove their worth. No one can be admitted to the inner circle, or higher mysteries of the Spiritual Life, and vested with power, until he has overcome himself and certain weaknesses of the flesh.

"For many are called, but few are chosen." Many who set out on the Path do not get very far—they fail at the tests. They find themselves vested with a certain amount of power, or they believe that they possess a certain amount of power, and then comes the temptation to misuse it. At this test many fail.

This, however, is not the first test by any means. Upon the first starting out upon the new life there is great joy and uplift. Everything goes smoothly and the neophyte is apt to think that there is nothing easier than living the life of the Spirit.

But, before long, the first test is met with. Everything appears to go wrong. Spiritual uplift goes and all the old passions, temptations and desires of the flesh return with added power. Every inducement is made to persuade the neophyte to return to the old life of the senses. This test is quite sufficient for a great many. They go ack to the old life, and, by so doing, prove themselves to be unworthy of higher responsibility. The higher mysteries are certainly not to be revealed to those who fail at the first hurdle.

The first test safely passed through, the sun again comes out and life is once more a joy. But old habits and passions still keep cropping up, and it is only by continually turning to the Spirit and drawing upon His inexhaustible powers that they can be overcome.

Apart from all these experiences connected with the overcoming of the lower nature, and the old desires, it is found, sooner or later, that subtle tests are, from time to time, being brought to bear upon one. If they are not dealt with in the right way; if we refuse to learn their lesson; or if we shirk the experience that they bring, because it entails trusting ourselves more completely than ever before to the Spirit and pushing out into much deeper waters; then the tests are applied again and again until their lessons are learnt and the weak point in our character built up and strengthened. When we have learnt our lesson, without a shadow of doubt, the tests are removed, and not before. When they are no longer necessary these particular tests are removed forever, and we are advanced another step in the new life, greater power and responsibilities being then given us.

After a time of rest and preparation, we are next subjected to a series of tests more strenuous, searching and subtle than previous ones. This is necessary, because, as we advance, the tests have to be of a different character and quality. The tests applied to an archangel must of necessity be of a very different character from those applied to a human being. In every case the tests are perfectly adapted to the individual soul. No one is tested or tempted beyond his powers. We can always overcome if we are faithful to the Light, refusing either to give way, or to turn our backs to the Light.

We proceed by a series of steps, each step being preceded by a testing time. All this takes place as we pursue our ordinary everyday duties.

Chapter 2

INITIATION (CONTINUED)

IN the previous chapter we stated that initiation rites and ceremonies, conducted when in a dream state, or when the soul is out of the body (trance), do not appear to be necessary, because we have discovered that life's experiences are the great Initiator. Since this was penned it has been brought to our notice that we are far from being alone in this opinion, as many of those who are learned in these matters are of the opinion that initiation tests are not the real thing, but are symbolic only of the experiences through which the soul must pass in everyday life. This is interesting, and may be helpful to many of our readers who have been looking forward to an elaborate and mystical initiation ceremony and series of tests, all the while being unaware that life itself is the great Initiator, and that the daily round and common task provide us with all the tests that are necessary.

It was a wonderful discovery to us when it was revealed to us by the Spirit that we are day by day being tested, and that our everyday life is nothing really in itself, but is a continuous trial, training and experience, leading up to various stages of initiation. It came to us more or less as a shock, for we felt that we had come up against one of the really great things, beside which all earthly events and ambitions fade into insignificance.

This discovery, or revelation, was of more importance than may appear to be the case to the reader who has not yet met with the same experience. It was important because it brought home to us, with startling vividness, the reality of the spiritual life. We knew then in a very real sense that we were really in the Path and that invisible forces were guiding us and leading us on. It was also important to us because it was also revealed to us that we had managed to pass certain tests over which we thought we had failed. This gave renewed hope and confidence, for it showed us that, in spite of apparent failure, by maintaining a steadfast mind and by keeping our face turned towards the Light, refusing to be stampeded by failure and sin and falling short of the Divine Ideal, we were winning through. Not by any might of our own, but by the Power of the Spirit. This proved to us that we had been proceeding along right lines. After years of failure, trying to fight evil and the lower nature, only to be worsted every time, we had come to the conclusion that the only way by which victory is possible is by turning to the Spirit, letting Him overcome for us. So long as we fight evil, ourselves, we are bound to be defeated, but when we turn to the Spirit and put ourselves in His hands, acknowledging that of ourselves we call do nothing, and that the battle is the Lord,s, we put ourselves on the side of victory. We may fail many times: we may stumble and fall frequently: we may appear to have failed miserably, but if we remain steadfast, saying: "this is God's battle and I will trust wholly in Him,'' the enemy finally retires discomfited.

In the external life of business, and what not, it is the man or woman who has a steadfast mind, and who refuses to be stampeded when everything appears to be lost, who wins through and becomes securely and substantially successful. In the spiritual life the same thing holds true. It is the steadfast soul who wins through.

An error into which we are all likely to fall is in thinking that we must be especially vile and wicked to be tempted in such ways as all are tempted at times. It is not evidence of our wickedness at all. The sin or wickedness or weakness is not in our being tempted, but in giving way to the temptation to give up the quest, to turn our backs on the Light, and to lose faith in the power and ability of the Spirit to bring us safely through. All these tests are necessary: they form part of our initiation. All the powers of darkness rise up and seek to overwhelm us, but it is, in a sense, a performance got up specially for our benefit. It is true that they would "down us" if they could, but, on the other hand, we could never "attain" if it were not for the tests that they give us.

No matter how many times we may fail, if we steadfastly keep our face turned towards the Light, we are bound to win through. Not through anything that we do ourselves, but because we remain steadfast in the One Eternal Spirit. As Whittler sings: "I know not where His islands lift Their fronded palms in air; I only know I cannot drift Beyond His love and care."

Chapter 3

THE QUEST

BECAUSE We are Divine children of our Father (Father-Mother, Wisdom-Love) God; and because we, like the prodigal son, have left our Father's house to wander in a far country (our journey through time and space, which includes our life on this plane) in order to gain wisdom, there is in each one of us an unconquerable longing for Home.

Home. What blessed memories cling to this word, even though we think only of the earthly home of our youth. The home of our youth is scattered—and the home which many of us have got together for our children will be scattered also—but our Father's House is eternal, forever calling us to return.

Deeply embedded in each soul is this longing for God and for Home. It is the origin of desire. It is this desire that makes men dissatisfied. If they are in one place they wish to be in another. As soon as they arrive at the other place, which seemed from a distance to be so desirable, they are still dissatisfied and want to go elsewhere. Others seek satisfaction in sex passion and other forms of sensation, or in human loves of the purest kinds. Some seek in high things and others in low, but in none of them is satisfaction to be found.

Desire is always driving man forward. Disappointed in one thing he tries another, but in none of them does he find satisfaction. They all bring pain and suffering.

Nothing is more elusive than the call of sex. It promises happiness, but gives only the ashes of disappointment. It is only when passion is replaced by the purer flame of a more spiritual love, that true and lasting domestic peace becomes possible.

People sometimes write to us saying they are unhappy in their marriage, and that they love someone else. What shall they do? How can they get a divorce? How can they use occult powers (they call them New Thought!) so as to bring someone of the opposite sex to their side'? Poor things! Still chasing rainbows and will-o'-the-wisps. Will they never learn wisdom? They are offended when they are told that if they try to satisfy their desire they will become still more unhappy; and that if they use mind domination they will literally destroy themselves.

Let it be said here that if mind powers are used (even in the form of prayer) to alter the objective life and to change one's circumstances, trouble and disharmony are increased thereby. Confusion is made worse confounded.

Yet man's power to love must not be repressed. It must be poured out to the utmost. A remedy for this is found in our Lord's words of infinite wisdom: "Thou shalt love the Lord thy God with all thy heart, and with all thy soul, and with all thy mind, and with all thy strength: . . . and thy neighbour as thyself. There is none other commandment greater than this."

Not love of self, not passion (mis-termed love), not even love of personalities, but love of the Whole, namely, God and our fellows. This does not mean that we are to love those near and dear to us less, but to love God and our fellows more.

Christ came not to give us our heart's desires (that is, desires for carnal or material things); neither was His mission to help us in chasing the baubles of life. He came to transmute our desire, so that we might seek after wisdom and Divine union, in which there are eternal joy, peace, satisfaction and felicity, instead of for the things which fade away.

Christ can raise us to the heights, where, with eyes opened by Divine Wisdom, we can look over the sea of life. Upon its surface are blown the gaily painted baubles of illusion that lure men on and on, and ever in vain. Eager hands clutch at them, then sink, only to make room for others just as deluded. But there is one—the Christ—who stands with arms outstretched to save, saying: ''Come unto me and I will give you rest.'' "Take my yoke upon you and learn of me: for I am meek and lowly in heart: and ye shall find rest for your souls.

" Today on the heights I stand Above the sea of thought, And look o'er the changing drift At the baubles for which men fought; That slip through their clinging hands And ever remain uncaught.

Unchained through the drift of years They float o'er the surface clear; And forever warm hands reach out As the illusions of life draw near: Till the weary hands sink deep And the eager new appear.

Today on the heights I stand Where God's winds sing lullaby, And no more I reach for the gleam Of the baubles for which men die— For I reach to the heart of God And master of fate am I.

—HENRY VICTOR MORGAN.

Chapter 4

THE INNER LIFE I

ONE by one the things which bind us to the world reveal themselves to the seeker as frauds and shams. They glitter and attract, but when we have paid a big price for them, they are found to be worthless and worse than useless.

One by one the dear earthly props, upon which we rested our hopes and pride, are removed, until we are left alone.

Alone with the fact that all earthly things fail to satisfy: that no human love or form can be held forever: that life itself is short and its little tide ebbing fast.

"Change and decay in all around I see. Oh! Thou who changest not, Abide with me."

If in the outward life all is change and decay: if life itself is short and transient: if death threatens to put an end to all things; where then is that which is permanent, real and satisfying, and the life that fades not away?

This life is the inner life. God's eternal life which can be possessed by the humble seeker, but which is not revealed to the proud and arrogant. "Except ye be converted, and become as little children, ye shall not enter into the kingdom of heaven." (Matt. xviii, 3.) The kingdom of heaven is the inner life. "The kingdom of God cometh not with observation: neither shall, they say: Lo here! or lo there! for, behold, the kingdom of God is within you". (Luke xvii, 2.)

Everything connected with spiritual things seems to be in the form of a paradox. In order to find the real (or inner) life, the seeker has to lose or give up the only life of which he has any practical knowledge or experience. "He that findeth his life shall lose it; and he that loseth his life for my sake shall find it."

By giving up the external life and its vanities, we find the inner life of the Spirit, which is eternal.

All life is wonderful. As we write this we are seated in the garden, and a "Daddy Long Legs" alights on our writing pad. He crawls over the paper as though to investigate the writing. What a wonderful piece of workmanship. What beautiful wings, what marvellous legs. Yet, how soon he dies! The daisies at our feet, how wonderful! Yet, how soon they fade! Wonderful? Yes. Beautiful? Yes. But where, O where, is the life that fades not away?

Behind all changing form we find a life that persists and repeats. This is God's life, but it is not the life we seek, for even this life, perpetual though it may appear to be, is not eternal. It will have an end when the universe is rolled up like a scroll, and heaven and earth pass away.

Paradoxically, while God is the author of all life and therefore, in one sense, all life is the life of God, yet the life that perishes is not, in another sense, God's life, in that God's eternal life transcends all lower forms of life. Creation is ever changing, yet behind it all stands the imperishable Idea, unaffected by time or change.

This interior, permanent reality is what we all seek. Only let us find this pearl of great price and we shall be satisfied.

We can find the inner life of Eternal Being only by being born again of the Spirit.

The Adam man is of the earth, earthy. The second man is the Lord from heaven.*

We have to become as little children before we can enter the kingdom of heaven and win the crown of life which fadeth not away.

*"As in Adam all die, even so in Christ shall all be made alive."(1 Cor. xv 22.)

We have to lose all our craft and worldly wisdom; all our arrogance and pride; all our love of pomp, power, show; all envy, hate, malice, covetousness; all claim, of ourselves, to know anything, to be able to do anything, to be anything. In other words, we have to surrender out torch of life to Christ. "O Light that followest all my way, I yield my flickering torch to Thee."

When we "lose" our life in this way, we discover the larger life of God—the life which alone satisfies, the life which alone is eternal. We lose nothing in reality— although we must be willing to lose all—for Christ fans the feeble spark of our torch into His own glorious flame, until Christ is all and in all. Then is Christ risen from the dead, in us, and we are raised to immortality in Him.

Our Lord is coming again. Not as a babe in weakness, but as a super-dimensional Being, Lord of Heaven and earth, who is able to appear "in the twinkling of an eye," in power.

It is only those who have cultivated the inner life, who will be glad at His appearing.

"And every eye shall see Him, and they also which pierced Him. And all kindreds of the earth shall wail because of Him."

Chapter 5

THE INNER LIFE II

ONE could say much about the inner life which would be intelligible to only a small percentage of our readers. We shall therefore say what we have to say very simply indeed, confining ourselves to the elementary aspects of a very big and deep subject.

By meditation, communion and real prayer it is possible to make contact with the secret Source of Life and Being. If we do this daily, in addition to living the life, rendering service to others, and doing the Will of "our Father in Heaven," we not only cultivate the spiritual life, but find, also, the real inner Eternel Life of God, or Kingdom of Heaven.

It is unnecessary to possess occult knowledge, to develop psychic powers, to be able to leave the body and visit other planes, to go into trances, to use breathing exercises, to indulge in mystical ecstasy, to receive messages from the other side, or to practise any complicated methods of so-called development, in order to find

the inner life. All that we have to do is to follow the teaching of the Supreme Teacher, the Lord from Heaven, outwardly manifested as Jesus Christ, and inwardly, as the Christos within in the soul, born not of the will of the flesh, but of the Spirit from above.

All complicated, wonderful, esoteric, psychic, occult and secret practices can be put on one side. They are not only unnecessary, but they may lead out of the true

Path. The Kingdom of God can be found simply through waiting upon God, finding the Christ within, bringing every thought and desire into captivity to Him, and by following the teachings of Jesus in our life and conduct.

Through quiet prayer and meditation the spiritual part of us becomes nourished and strengthened. The Christ Child within grows according to the amount of spiritual nourishment It receives through our quiet waiting upon God. Every time that we turn to the Divine Father we draw strength from above. The Christ Child within grows and expands until He takes entire charge of our life; then the old self is obliterated and we know it no more. Through prayer and meditation, by right thinking, plus right living, an entire transformation takes place. The character becomes completely changed. We become new creatures, not after the likeness of the imperfect Adam, who is of the earth, earthy: but after the pattern of the perfect Christ, the Lord from Heaven.

The Kingdom of God is not to be found, neither can the inner life be nourished, by the feverish reading of many books, the attendance at lectures, the vain rushing after first this teacher and then that, nor by listening merely to fine sermons, but only by quiet waiting upon God in the secret place, and by living the Christ life day by day.

"But thou, when thou prayest, enter into thy inner chamber, and having shut thy door, pray to thy Father which is in secret, and thy Father which seest in secret shall recompense thee."

By retiring into the quiet chamber of the soul: by shutting the door upon external things, and by communing with our spiritual Father, we touch the One Source of all Life, becoming quickened by the Spirit and filled with Divine Power.

No one who does not practise this inner secret communion with his Spiritual Source can ever keep alive the flame of his inner life. Many start out upon the great quest with joy and enthusiasm, but comparatively few finish the course. So many fall by the wayside. They lose interest, become cold, and go back to the "beggarly elements of the world". The reason is, in every case, that they neglect the inner communion with the Father in secret. They think that they can do without it.

They think, perhaps, that public prayer will do instead, or that a few statements of Truth repeated during the day will do just as well. These things, good and necessary though they be, can never take the place of the inner, secret communion with the Author of our being. Without the daily meeting with God in meditation, contemplation and true prayer, the inner Life languishes and dies. The one who was so enthusiastic over spiritual things goes back to the old life, but never to find either happiness or satisfaction again. One glimpse of the higher, richer and fuller life of the Spirit: only one short experience of the power of the risen life of Christ, makes it impossible for us ever to be satisfied with the baubles of the world and the selfish pleasure of sin. No matter how madly we may plunge into pleasure; no matter how deeply we may drink of its intoxicating draught; we can never forget—the worm dieth not.

Well do I remember—and every time I think of him it gives my heart an ache—one who, with the writer, years ago, publicly acknowledged himself to be a convert to

Christianity, and an avowed follower of Jesus Christ. No one can publicly confess the name of' Jesus Christ as his Lord without receiving a blessing. But this man seemed to receive a double portion. I never remember seeing anyone so lifted up and exalted. His face glowed with the Light of the Spirit. His voice was tremulous with joy as he told us that everything spoke to him of God, even the leaves of the trees shouted aloud His name.

But the uplift went, as it always does, and this man went down, as we all have to do, into the wilderness to be tempted. He neglected the secret place: he thought he could do without prayer: he lost touch with his Divine Source: his spiritual life became dried up and withered at the roots.

In time he went back to the old life. Drink claimed him as a victim. But, no matter how much he might drink, he was not happy. He was not happy even in his cups, but only quarrelsome. Finally, he committed suicide.

And when I think of that time when the voice of his Beloved was heard even in the whispering of the trees, I could weep, and doubtless would do so, did I not believe that God is able to overrule everything for good, and to save even that poor soul out of its wretchedness and woe. When I heard the sad news of his tragic passing, I said: "There goes H. T. H., but for the Grace of God." We are all backsliders, more or less, but God is able to save even to the uttermost.

Such a sad history as this only makes one the more anxious to warn all and sundry that the inner life can be cultivated only to the extent that we wait upon God and commune with Him, as spirit with Spirit, in the secret place.

Chapter 6

THE INNER LIFE III

"IF you want to know the way, ask the one who has travelled it," is a wise saying.

If we would learn how to tread the Path of Attainment we must go to the One who has successfully passed through it. Entrance to the Kingdom of God is not to be found through a mere assent to creeds and dogmas. They may be true and sound enough, but they cannot save. If we are to learn how to climb the steep ascent to God we must go to the One who has already climbed it, and has prepared the way for us. This One is Jesus Christ.

By examining His life and living a life like it, and not only hearing (or reading) His sayings, but doing them, thus becoming doers of the word and not hearers only, we find the inner secret path which admits us to eternal life, or the Kingdom of God.

About the teaching of Jesus we must speak later, but about what Jesus did, the most outstanding thing is our Lord's dependence upon prayer and communion with the Unseen. Jesus did not attain to mastery over His human self and its weaknesses, the powers of darkness, and the forces of nature, by idle wishing; neither was it given to Him without any seeking on His part. Having taken upon Himself all our weaknesses and limitations, our Lord had to win His way into the Kingdom of the Higher Consciousness in just the same way that we have to do, viz., by prayer, meditation, and communion with the Unseen.

Jesus would not have attained if He had neglected the inner life and been satisfied with five minutes spent in prayer night and morning. He spent hours and whole nights in prayer. If it had not been necessary Christ would never have spent all this time in prayer, for it would have been a waste of time. The fact that Jesus spent so much time in meditation is, we think, the best possible proof that much prayer and communion was necessary.

If prayer was a vital necessity in the case of Jesus, it is, to say the least, equally necessary to each one of us who would seek to scale the heights of spiritual attainment. Yet how much time do we spend, each day, in prayer, meditation and communion?

It is true that by making use of the Mental Law of Association it is possible to condense what might take hours of meditation into, say, half an hour; but how many are prepared to spend even that short space of time, night and morning, in the Quiet Place?

Better a short time than none at all. Far better to spend only five minutes in real touch with our Divine Source than to neglect communion altogether, for this will save our spiritual life from entire extinction. But how much better to spend as much time as possible in the Secret Place, where, by making contact with our Divine Source, we draw upon inexhaustible fountains of Life, Wisdom and Power!

Not enough time, the reader may say. It may seem so, but it is our experience that if we neglect meditation and prayer, either for sleep or work, we are the losers thereby. The extra sleep does us no good, and no more work seems to get done, while that which is done deteriorates in quality. On the other hand, if we go without sleep in order to pray, we never miss it, or suffer any ill effects; while our work still gets done, and done more easily, at the same time being of more value to others.

Chapter 7

THE INNER LIFE IV

IT does not matter how "tangled up" our life may be, nor how filled with disharmony and trouble, if we make daily use of the secret place for quiet meditation upon, and communion with, our Divine Source, everything will, in time, become harmoniously adjusted. Divine Order is inherent and is the reality. The disorders of life are due to a violation of Divine Law which causes a disturbance or rupture.

This disturbance subsides when we cease producing it. We cease producing disharmony when we turn to God and meditate upon His Divine Perfections. The effect of meditation is to change us into the likeness of that upon which we meditate. It is easy to recognize one who practises daily meditation. The face is calm and spiritual, showing forth the fruits of the Spirit rather than the desires of the flesh. For the reason that we cease disturbing the Divine Order and violating Divine Law, and, instead, meditate upon the one Source of Harmony, the disorders of life cease. The inherent Divine Order appears of its own accord, as a natural consequence.

It is only by the cultivation of the Inner Life that the outer life can be made harmonious, happy, and truly successful.

All attempts at altering the external life by means of mind power, mental." treatments," or even prayer, only have the effect of making "confusion worse confounded''. It is a good many years since mental science and similar vogues started, and the adherents of these various cults are now to be numbered in millions, yet the world is as diseased and discordant as ever. Such people have continually to be making what they term "demonstrations". As soon, however, as one "demonstration" has been made it becomes necessary to make another. And so the weary business for ever repeats itself.

Through lack of wisdom it is possible for one possessed of a certain amount of knowledge and power in prayer, or "treatment," to go on making "demonstration" after "demonstration," each one not in accordance with the Divine plan of his life, until at last there is a terrible catastrophe which sweeps everything into ruins.

Without wisdom we are far more likely to ''demonstrate'' that which is quite the wrong thing for us than that which is the right, consequently the more "demonstrations" are made, the greater becomes the disorder of the life.

Contrast this unsatisfactory and futile method with that of true meditation upon God, the Cause of all Harmony, Wholeness and Perfection, or, rather, Who is these things, and the advantage of the latter is at once seen. By meditating upon God, finding Him in the Secret Place, the Presence of the Most High, into which mortals, who are sufficiently in earnest and pure in motive, and who can be trusted, may enter, the inner life becomes harmoniously adjusted, so that it conforms to the Divine Order of the Spirit. The natural consequence of this being that Divine order and harmony become reflected in the external life.

This does not mean that we are not to take our troubles and difficulties to God, but rather the reverse. If we take them into the Secret Place and meditate upon God as Wisdom, Guidance, and so on, allowing God a free hand to solve our problems in His own way, and being willing to be led entirely by the Spirit, everything works together for good and the only possible right course is taken.

The great error we are at first prone to fall into is in jumping to the conclusion that we must have this thing, or that, in order to get free from certain limitations and irksome conditions, and in using all our mental and spiritual powers and the great power of prayer in an endeavour to bring to us the thing which we think we must have.

What we think we must have is probably the worst possible thing for our happiness and well-being. If we succeed in demonstrating it, great disorder and unhappiness are the result, and it seems necessary to make more and more demonstrations. On the other hand, if we are not successful in "demonstrating" that which we think we must have, we are unhappy because we cannot have what we think is vitally necessary, and our whole life is filled with failure and discord, because all our energies are directed into a wrong channel.

Instead of saying that we must have this thing or that we should go to the Fount of all Wisdom, and by meditation become filled with wisdom not our own, so that we are led to do the only wise thing, and to take the only right course possible in the circumstances.

Chapter 8

THE INNER LIFE V

WE have already seen that the cultivation of the inner life is the only way to harmony and peace. But even of greater importance is the fact that without this we can never overcome all that wars against our spiritual growth and progress, nether can we "grow" our spiritual body without which, when our "earthly" body is cast off, we should be found naked. No one, of course, can manufacture his own spiritual body. Like Eternal Life itself, it is the gift of God, but the spiritual body grows and develops only to the extent that we cultivate our spiritual character.

While salvation is of God through Christ, we have to work out our own salvation with fear and trembling. The spiritual body is a Divine growth or development, but it needs care, attention, and cultivation. No gardener, it does not matter how clever be may be, can make a flower grow of itself. He cannot give it life, for this is from God, but he can cultivate it. He can remove the weeds, water the flower, see that the sunshine reaches it, and give it extra nourishment. As a result of his care a beautiful and healthy plant is produced, but the life and inherent beauty come from God.

It is the same with our spiritual body. it is the gift of God, but it comes to us only as we cultivate the inner life.

Therefore, the cultivation of the inner life should be our principal aim. All the experiences of life should be looked upon as helps to the development of a truly spiritual and Christ-like character. Our aim should not be our own comfort, but rather to bring forth the fruits of the Spirit, which are: love, joy, peace, long-suffering, gentleness, goodness, faith, meekness, temperance. So long as we seek merely for comfort, trying at all times to make life easier and pleasanter for ourselves, we make life more difficult and delay our own spiritual growth.

Life is the great initiator. Life's problems are the stepping stones which lead to attainment. Each problem is perfectly arranged to provide us with the experience that we need in order to make the next step upward along the spiritual path.

When we have overcome our immediate problem, we have built something permanently into our spiritual character—we have added something to our eternal spiritual body.

Character is the only thing that endures. Our spiritual body is the objective expression on spiritual planes of our spiritual character. Therefore, by developing character we build up our spiritual body—the body which alone can supply us with a vehicle of expression on spiritual planes, through the aeons, or eternity.

Problems and difficulties, then, instead of being looked upon as evil or as nuisances, must be met as friends who have come to help us into the Kingdom of God—to the wedding feast, at which we have to wear the wedding garment (spiritual body). Whatever our problem, grief, perplexity, difficulty or painful experience may be, it is the best thing for us at the time. Some lack of character within has called them into being and we can get rid of the problem or difficulty only as we ourselves become inwardly changed.

Our aim, then, when meeting difficulty, should be not to overcome in order to have a pleasant and enjoyable time again, but in order to develop the special quality of character that is demanded of us. Therefore all problems and difficulties should be taken into the Silence and spread out before God, so that the Spirit who is guiding us in our journey towards Divine Union, can show us where we are wrong, what weaknesses must be overcome, or wrong attitude of mind changed.

By looking upon life's experiences as helps in the life of spiritual attainment; by seeking within for wisdom; by devoting a set time each day to meditation; by connecting ourselves up to the Spirit throughout the day by means of affirmations of Truth; by these means we build up Christian Character, thus preparing for our use the spiritual body—which is the gift of God, nevertheless—that shall be the vehicle of expression for our use through the aeons on celestial planes.

Chapter 9

TESTS

A READER in South Africa asks: "Why do those who set out to live the life of the Spirit meet, before long, with such setbacks and discouragements? It seems unfair that those who make no effort to live a higher life are not opposed in this way, while those who try to do good and be good have to meet and overcome tests and trials."

This has always been the case. There is only one Path really, although each seeker of the Kingdom may think that he is travelling a different one. For instance, the modern seeker, calling himself New Thought, Divine Science, or what not, may think that he is following a different and—let us whisper it!—superior path to that travelled by, say, John Bunyan, but he is not. It is the same Path, and, in John Bunyan's Pilgrim's Progress you will find a description of all the difficulties and tests that the soul has to meet, written in some of the most charming and beautiful English that has ever been penned. And John Bunyan was an uneducated tinker! Which proves that he was inspired by the Spirit when he wrote his immortal work.

Because there is only one Path, along which all must travel, saviour, master, initiate, saint, and ordinary people such as we, all seekers of the Kingdom of God are subject to the same laws. The most "modern" thinker has to pass through precisely the same experiences as did those of old. By no amount of thought-power can anyone avoid a single test or experience; but, by his steadfastness, he can overcome where others of weaker resolve would fail.

When we first set out on the Path, having decided with a glad heart to give our whole lives to God, and to make the search for the Kingdom our principal aim, we go along very swimmingly for a time. We are intensely happy and lifted up.

It seems so easy, too, tripping light-heartedly along the Path in this way, without a cloud in the sky, rejoicing in the freedom and liberty of the Spirit. Old temptations seem to be left behind forever; weaknesses appear to be overcome once and for all; while delightful spiritual influences seem to be attending our way. We sing with a glad heart the early part of the twenty-third Psalm, but cannot understand the verse referring to the valley of the shadow.

But, after a time, we come to our first hurdle. It is not going to be such an easy thing as we imagined. The hurdle appears to be too high for any human being to jump, or even climb, over. Here is a setback—no thoroughfare! If we try to find a path round the obstacle we become landed in much greater difficulties. Evidently there is no way round; either we must overcome the difficulty or go back to the place from which we have come. Which is it to be? To go on, even if it be possible, seems to lead to nothing but trouble, difficulty, darkness, and danger. Looking back we can see the alluring lights of the City from which we came—the City of Destruction. In the distance we can hear sounds of revelry and the banging of doors. Here we are, out in the darkness of the cold night with an apparently insuperable barrier in front of us, and beyond that—what? What is the use of trying to go on? Why not go back and be comfortable instead of suffering in this unpleas
ant way?

WHICH IS IT TO BE?

This is the first test. You all know the result. Those who are not in earnest, who are not fired by a resolve that no opposition can conquer, and a desire for the Kingdom that no discouragement can quench, go back from whence they came.

They have proved their unsuitability for the stern life of spiritual attainment, that they are not fit to scale the heights of God. For such let the incense of our prayers ascend, for they need all the help that we can give. But those who are in earnest, those whose whole desire is fixed upon God, who will not falter, who refuse to go back, and who are prepared to die in their tracks, if necessary, rather than give up the quest, these are the ones who go forward. Nothing can stop them, for there is no power in heaven or hell that can stop a soul aflame with the desire to find the Kingdom and to see God. When the test is completed, and the steadfastness of the aspiring soul proved, the obstacle melts away and the victorious march is resumed.

And so we go on. Before each step forward there is the time of test and discipline.

And it is well that it is so.

Chapter 10

LOVE, THE MAGIC KEY

LOVE is life and hate is death, shall we not choose the Path of Life? Love is the magic key that unlocks the doors of heaven. We do not have to ask for love, but only to give it—to express it. Love is the supreme law of life: guided by Wisdom it rules the universe. Every thought, every desire, every word, every emotion that is not Love, or which is against Love, or is out of harmony with the Law of Love, creates disorder, suffering, discord, ugliness, unhappiness, from which there is no escape. "Whatsoever a man soweth that shall he also reap." Nothing is truer than this—that we are mixed up with the disorder of our own sowing, that we cannot escape from it, except we make the supreme surrender to the Law of Love, and bring every thought, word, deed, and desire into captivity to it.

We are so slow to learn. Our Lord came so long ago to teach us this wonderful gospel of love. Have we learnt it? Have we surrendered to it? Have we obeyed it?

Have the nations of the earth obeyed it? Alas, no. This gospel is so simple, yet so difficult. Only to love—that is all. Two thousand years of Christian teaching, and yet look at the nations today! So little love, but so much suspicion and hatred, jealousy and envy. Instead of following the Lord of Love have we not made Him a scapegoat, by which we might save our miserable souls and get to heaven, no matter what might happen to others? No creed or dogma, or theological theory, good and necessary though it be, can ever take the place of the complete surrender to, and the sincere following of, the Lord of Love.

We said just now that we cannot evade the consequence of our sowing. That if we sow seeds of hate, indifference, coldness, ill-will, selfishness, envy, or anything that is out of harmony with Divine Love, we must of necessity reap an appropriate harvest. If a farmer sowed weeds instead of corn, no matter how much he might pray about the matter, the crop that he would reap would be weeds and not corn.

In the same way, so long as we sow to the flesh, with its hates and lusts, we reap disharmony and corruption. When, however, we surrender to the Lord of Love and follow Him, no matter where He may lead: when we establish our life on the Principle of Love: when we obey to the uttermost the dictates of the Law of Love, we not only cease sowing seeds of suffering and discord, but also the Divine Order begins to manifest in our life and affairs. This is because we cease fighting against the trials, troubles, sufferings, and disciplines which we have brought upon ourselves, and leave off rebelling against the sorrowful experiences of life which are the result of sin against Love's law; and, instead, co-operate with life's experiences, transmuting them so that they become a source of blessing instead of a curse or scourge.

The Path of Attainment is the Way of Love. It is the Path our Lord has trodden before us. We can but follow in His blessed footsteps, along the hallowed way of Love and Service. Love to all, service to all; self being forgotten and left behind.

Chapter 11

HOW TO MEET LIFE'S DIFFICULTIES AND PERPLEXITIES

THE spiritual life is beset with problems and difficulties. If a student is fairly advanced his life is free from the disorder produced by wrong thinking and through acting against the harmony of the Divine Order, but he has to pass through a series of initiations, each one bringing him nearer to the Heart of Divine Being. Pilgrims of the Path are like children at school. They have to pass through examination after examination in order to test their fitness for promotion to higher classes. As Olive Mercer says in her beautiful book, Life Transcendent, "Tests are fitted to each individual. No one would complain about his fiery ordeals did he but realize how necessary they are for him at certain stages of unfoldment. We call our own initiations upon us by knocking at the door of a higher classroom. Impatiently we want to enter a bigger school of experience, but first we must show our certificate.

We must prove that we have the ability to cope with life's small experiences before we are allowed to rush recklessly through new doors. Is anyone ready to sail the high seas when it fills him with terror to cross the sheltered harbour?''

Many, therefore, are the perplexities which come to the traveller along the Path of Spiritual Attainment, and each one of them is necessary. Each experience is exactly the test that we require at the time in order to prepare us for what lies before us, to test our fitness or worthiness, and, most important of all, to bring us a step nearer to the Heart of Being.

One who has realised the great truth that life consists of a series of initiations and that each experience is necessary and exactly suited for the needs of the moment, such never complains of life's experiences. He may not welcome difficult or perplexing circumstances with enthusiasm, but he never complains or finds fault.

For one thing, he knows that he will come safely through them if he is patient and steadfast, looking to God, and trusting entirely to the Spirit in the face of seeming disaster or apparently insuperable difficulty.

In spite of this knowledge, born of experience by the way, the pilgrim at times finds his path very dark and his burden of perplexities about as much as he can bear. The great thing to do at these times is to go right up to the difficulty. Suffering, terror, anxiety, are due to an unwillingness to meet the trouble or difficulty. When, however, we walk right up to it, knowing that we can be led only to our highest good, the threatened evil passes away, and Divine Love and Wisdom stand revealed.

A short time ago a student of Truth wrote to us in great trouble. Terrible things were looming ahead, and the burden of the letter was: "How can I escape this threatened trouble?" Our reply was: "Take hold of God's hand and go right up to the trouble, meeting it bravely instead of trying to avoid it." The next letter told us that our advice had been followed, and the threatened trouble had turned out to be Love in disguise.

This advice may sound absurdly simple, suitable only for Sunday School children, but we were able to offer it only because we had learnt its truth through actual experience. At one time we were faced with a situation which filled us with dismay, if not actual terror. When, however, like a flash, we realized that we could be led only to that which is good, and when we surrendered entirely to God, asking Him to lead us wherever He willed, for wherever it might be, it could be only for our real and highest good, when this realization came to us our trouble faded away, and rest and peace descended upon us, filling our soul with great thankfulness, peace, and joy.

There is another object in perplexing and trying experiences, but this must be described in our next chapter.

Chapter 12

SERVING OTHERS

WHILE it is true that man may reduce the disorder of his own life almost to vanishing point by bringing his thoughts into harmony with Truth, he yet may be mixed up with the troubles of others. Indeed, his greater capacity to love and serve others may bring him experiences which he would otherwise not meet. As a matter of fact, he does not want to avoid them, for the one idea of the advanced soul is to serve others and to deal faithfully, day by day, with the problems and experiences that life brings to him. His principal sorrow may not have anything to do with his own life, but may be concerned with the life of another. Someone whom he loves may be in trouble, or may be taking the wrong path in life. We all of us, at some time, have to pass through such experiences as these. The troubles of others may cause us more suffering than anything that could befall us personally. It is our privilege to know a saintly soul of a man—a clergyman —who bears on his own shoulders the troubles and griefs of all his parishioners who will allow him to share their sorrows. Whenever the wings of the Dark Angel cast their shadow over a home there is a knock at the door—it is the Vicar come to pray with the bereaved and to tell them of life beyond the grave, in such a way as to take away forever all fear of death, and to lessen very sensibly the wrench of parting.

If there is pain to be borne, the Vicar is always close at hand. It does not matter at what inconvenience, nor how fatigued he may be, nothing can keep him away.

No wonder that to meet such a man as this makes one say: "This surely is not an ordinary man such as we, but a great soul come specially to earth to comfort and bless erring, suffering humanity, and lead them to higher and better things."

But even we who are of ordinary clay can get mixed up in things and not know where to turn because of the troubles of others. "What may be the good of it all?" you may say: "cannot we ever get a quiet time, free from experiences?" The "good of it" is that such experiences enrich the spiritual life, and through them we learn to know God better and in a more personal and intimate way than ever before.

One such personal experience may illustrate what we mean.

One night the burden of someone else's troubles and difficulties lay heavily upon us. Indeed, they had pressed upon us for days and weeks, but at this time the burden seemed very great. The whole night was spent, more or less, in prayer. Our soul was sad, for we seemed to come in contact with certain lives and yet we could influence them so little for good. Life seemed so empty and futile, because of the little good that we could do. Souls come in contact with us and then pass out into the night; and we seem to have influenced them so little, if at all. And so our heart went up in intercession. Was there no way of escape for this one? Could nothing be done to help? Then when it seemed that we had been humbled, to the depths, by a vision of our worthlessness and uselessness in the world, and of how far short we had fallen of that which we ought to have been; when we had been grieved and saddened beyond words by what apparently lay before the one with

whose trouble we were "mixed up," so to speak, God gave a sign, a gracious word
that brought peace to the soul. The words: "Cast thy burden on the Lord and He shall sustain thee. He shall never suffer the righteous to be moved," came into consciousness, with that wonderful sense of illumination and understanding that always accompany experiences of this kind. Such simple experiences as these are like hearing a voice from heaven. These words revealed to us the glorious fact that if we only put the whole trouble upon God, He would not only sustain us, but would sort everything out, unravel the tangled skein-although beyond hope from a human point of view—and over-rule everything for good.

The result of such an experience as this is to know God better than ever before, and to realize His Power and Presence more than ever before. And so we go on, ever making fresh discoveries of the richness and wonders of the love and care of

God.

Chapter 13

LIFE WITHOUT STRAIN I

WE often meet with good Christian people who are obviously bearing, or are trying to bear, all the troubles of the world on their own shoulders. Indeed, we, ourselves, may be more or less prone to the same weakness. The strain of bearing the burden of the whole world, or even of our own work, or the duties and responsibilities of life, is enormous, yet totally unnecessary.

Whether we are crushed to earth and worn out by the responsibilities of life, or are but little affected by them, depends entirely on our point of view. If we look at life as something that is evil, or that is always liable to go wrong, and which can be kept right only by our constant unwearying attention and care, anxiety, and strain, our burden becomes too great, almost, to be borne. But this is an entirely wrong idea of life. Life is not something evil, neither is it liable to go wrong at any time if we do not prevent it by strain and effort. Life is just the reverse of this. Life is good: it is the outcome of Love, and as always trying to bring good to us, if we will only allow it to do so.

Countless thousands must have worried themselves into their graves through this misunder- standing about life. Having read evil into everything, they expect evil to come to them, and what they have expected has come upon them. Fearing calamities at every turn of the road, they have suffered as much as they would have done if the calamities had really appeared, or even more so, for suspense is harder to bear than the actual calamity itself. Oh, the worry and the strain of life when it is looked at from the wrong angle!

Again, when disciplinary experiences come to such as we have been describing—for we all must have our griefs, sorrows, and dark times—when these come, they are met as evil happenings and fought and resisted tooth and nail. Oh, the strain and the suffering experienced by those who cannot say "Thy Will be done"!

Resistance and tension are the cause of strain. Most people today are suffering from strain. Christians and non-Christians, religious and irreligious, alike. Yet the Christian should never suffer from strain. Our Lord's teaching, if rightly ap-prehended, does away with strain. Christ's teaching is in perfect harmony and agreement with modern science. The latter teaches those suffering from nervous strain to relax instead of to resist. For instance, a nervous person may suffer horribly because of a certain noise. He is now taught to relax to the cause of annoyance instead of resisting it. When he does so his suffering ceases. Christ taught trust and rest in the love of the Father. He tells us to take no anxious thought about the morrow, neither to be anxious about supply of the necessary and good things of life. Why does our Lord speak thus? Simply because He knows that all is well, in reality, and that everything works together for good if we will only allow it to do so. The Divine Order is inherent, but we do not let it manifest itself because of our strained and anxious thought.

It must not be imagined, however, that being care-free, and relaxed, and without strain, is being careless and slothful. Letting things drift only makes matters worse. Refusing to face the difficulties of life leads only to great troubles. We have to meet our difficulties boldly, and then find ease and rest in God. When we do this systematically, Divine Guidance becomes ours, and everything works together for good in a wonderful manner.

Students should affirm in the face of seeming calamity, disaster, or trouble, that because God is the One Source of all, therefore nothing but good can come to them. Then go forward, meeting the trouble willingly and without resistance.

When we cease to resist, the strain disappears.

Chapter 14

LIFE WITHOUT STRAIN II

THE great fallacy to which we are all slaves, more or less, is the belief that we, of ourselves, have to do everything. At first we honestly think that we do have to accomplish everything ourselves, and are confident that we can do it without any help. This stage is probably necessary, for we all have to learn self-reliance and develop self-confidence, before we can pass on to the much higher stage of entire dependence upon God. But there comes a time when we are not as sure that we, of ourselves, can do everything. Indeed there comes a time when we realize that, of ourselves, we can do nothing. Most students think, when they meet with this experience, that they must have gone wrong somewhere. But this is not the case; it is all part of their normal unfoldment and initiation into higher things.

Life without strain becomes possible to the extent that we realize that God is doing everything and not we. Instead of saying: "I can do this, God helping me," we say "God is doing this thing and the most that I can do is to co-operate with Him."

The more we allow God to work through us the less strain there is in life. We do not have to plan, strive and strain to achieve, but simply allow the perfect Divine Plan concerning our life to unfold. Indeed, life becomes a process of unfoldment instead of a series of strenuous achievements. We have no fear for the future, for God is looking after this. All that we have to do is to live one day at a time, dealing as faithfully as possible with each experience, every one of which we have ourselves attracted; every one of which also is necessary, and has for its aim our highest good.

As the writer pens these words in his open-air shelter, it is raining. A tiny fly or gnat, so small as to be almost a mere speck, flies in, has a look round, and then flies out again into the rain. Apparently he flies between the drops. He is so small that one drop of rain, if it were to hit him, would hurl him to earth. But, apparently, he flies between the drops. If this be so what a strain upon the poor gnat's brain and nervous system such a performance would be, if he had to do it all! But he doesn't. Assuming that he does fly between the drops, he must do it by instinct.

Therefore, it is no strain or worry to him.

In the summer time, as the writer writes in his garden, the activities of ants and bees often arouse his interest. What a terrible worry it would be to the ants or bees if they had to sit down and plan how to build their anthills or nests! But they do no such thing. They do not think, worry, or strain, but obey the guidance of a greater mind which plans and carries out the whole undertaking.

It is not suggested that man can work by instinct, neither is it desirable that he should do so, or be a mere puppet. But he can pass through, by degrees, the stages of achievement, first by his own will, next by enlisting the help of God; and then finally to learn to let the Spirit of God work through him, so that the Divine Will is perfectly expressed. The more he can do so, the less the worry, care, strain, and effort. Such things as nervous breakdowns become things of the past.

It must not be thought, however, that this final stage can be reached all at once, or that it is at all possible to beginners. A beginner attempting it would increase his difficulties. It is beneficial to the more advanced worker, but harmful to the beginner. For instance, this article is being written without any effort or strain at all; yet the writer is, in the ordinary way, so slow at writing, and to him composition is so difficult, that even to compose a letter is a heavy task, only attempted because of a strong sense of duty.

Again, because he realizes that he is being led by the Spirit, the writer does not have to worry over decisions. When we are led by the Spirit all our decisions are right decisions, therefore there is no need to worry at all as to whether they are right or wrong. But, again, we must warn beginners that this is not possible at first. If a beginner attempted this he would probably lose all will-power and ability to make a decision.

Another word of warning.

Being led by the Spirit of God is not being controlled by spirits.

Therefore, we must first develop a strong and positive condition of mind and soul.

We must be sure that we make ourselves receptive to God alone. The door must be closed firmly to all but God and Christ. Therefore we have to develop a very positive attitude in every direction, except towards God and Christ. To Christ and Christ alone we can open ourselves completely, allowing Him to possess us utterly and entirely.

No one who is negative and dependent, or who has not overcome fear (that is, passed through the fear initiation) should attempt allowing the Spirit to work through him as a passive instrument.

Let it be understood also that allowing God the Spirit to work through us is not to indulge in automatic writing or any similar dangerous practice. This is the very negation of the real thing. It is accomplished by becoming negative to the very forces and powers towards which we should be positive, and against which we should be as strong as a rock.

Neither do we advocate the emptying of oneself and allowing just anything to fill us. To empty oneself negatively is a dangerous practice, and must be firmly avoided.

Christ taught the care-free life (not the careless life) of utter dependence upon God. The more we enter into Truth, the less care and strain there is in life.

Our Lord said that He did not do the works, but that the Father did them through Him, In the same way we can allow the Spirit to guide us, and to work through us, without strain or fatigue on our part. But we must attain to this stage gradually and by degrees. We must learn to know our Lord in an intimate and personal way by passing through certain experiences. These all come to us at the right time and in their natural sequence.

Chapter 15

LIFE WITHOUT STRAIN III

THERE is a deep inner truth which is sometimes hinted at, but is never clearly and plainly expressed in words. It is a truth that is too deep for words or finite definitions. It has sometimes been spoken of as "achievement without effort."

The secret was known to Lao Tsze, and today it is engaging some of our greatest minds. But they will never solve it through the intellect, but they may do so through intuition. Intuition belongs to the same order as this so-called "achievement without effort." It no doubt belongs to the world of four dimensions, or rather the consciousness of four or many dimensions. It belongs to the same order as those "happenings" that we call miracles. What it really is is so far beyond us as to make our brain reel if we attempt to understand it intellectually.

Although we cannot understand it, we can, however, know it, inwardly. By intuition, or an inward spiritual revelation, we can know and make contact with that which is entirely beyond the greatest human intellect. For instance, a simple unlearned person can know God and commune with Him inwardly through prayer, but what human intellect, no matter how profound, can understand Him? It is the same with the secret of effortless achievement, we may know how to use it and enjoy it, but we can never understand it intellectually.

There is an inner Divine Order which is the Reality and is always present. Everything that is not Reality has to disappear in the face of Reality. As soon as we leave off striving and resisting, becoming sufficiently quiet and receptive, the Divine Order appears. It is the Reality and must appear as soon as we become quiet enough. "In quietness . . . shall be your strength." "Be still and know that I am God."

There is an inner realm of quietness to which, when we are sufficiently advanced, we may penetrate. The one who wrote or dictated the 91st Psalm knew all about it. But this inner secret place of calm is not only a place of safety, it also causes things to come to pass, in what we may truthfully call a miraculous manner. By miraculous we mean transcending ordinary physical and natural law.

In order to make use of this unknown law or power, we have first to give up all effort, especially mental effort. When we are surrounded by every possible difficulty, trouble, complication and confusion, if we give up our hopeless, fatiguing, wearying efforts, and sit down quietly and be still, thinking and knowing only God, letting everything else go, utterly and completely, then absolute stillness comes to the soul, and the peace which passeth all understanding possesses our minds.

All that we have to do is just to become quite still and know God. We have not to do anything else. All that is necessary is to let go so completely that our mind becomes as placid as a motionless lake. Just as when a lake is quite still it reflects perfectly the surrounding beauty of hill and sky, so also does our mind, when perfectly calm, reflect the beauty, harmony, perfection and order of the Divine. When we become completely still, our mind becomes attuned to the Infinite Mind, after which nothing else matters.

It does not matter how complicated our troubles may be, nor how many or difficult our tasks, if we become quiet, as already described, the whole of our life and work becomes perfectly adjusted. Whatever is discordant "passes in music out of sight". Whatever is complicated becomes simple. Whatever is obscure becomes plain. Whatever seems impossible becomes easy of achievement. No matter how great one's responsibilities, life becomes almost as easy as "falling off a log."

How demoralizing! the uninitiated may say. It would be, no doubt, if the uninitiated could get within a hundred miles of it. But there is no fear of such a thing coming to pass. What we are speaking about has only, apparently, been known, in the past, to the most advanced souls of the race and there is even now no danger of beginners ever being able to use it. It is probably the most difficult thing in the spiritual life to enter the inner stillness in which we make actual contact with God. By the time that we can practise this most difficult art we are incapable of being demoralized by it. The sceptre of power is not given to the uninitiated, neither are the mysteries of the Kingdom of God revealed unto the neophyte.

Apart from this it is so difficult, in one sense, to find this inner place of calm, and become sufficiently quiet to be attuned to it, that all who are not sufficiently advanced would far rather go on toiling and struggling, even though hopelessly, rather than attempt it.

We said just now that to be quiet and still, simply sitting and resting passively in the Divine Light and Presence, letting everything go, is Probably the most difficult thing in the spiritual life. It is difficult because we feel that something must be done. We feel that if we do not pray or strive for this, that or the other, or for this loved one or that person, and so on, they will suffer, or something will go wrong.

We have to give up this finite idea entirely. Nothing of the kind is necessary. All that we have to do is to let go completely and know God. All sorts of cares and anxieties may claw at us, attempting to gain our attention, and numberless fears assail us, but they must all be brushed aside, everything must be let go, until at last we are perfectly quiet and still in the Divine Presence. When once we are able to relax in this way and be quite still and free, and severed from everything, then the miraculous can happen, and the apparently impossible be brought to pass.

The spiritual life is one long series of paradoxes, and this is one of them. The most difficult thing in the world is to be still, yet it makes life simple and easy. It removes all its cares, solves all its problems, takes away all its fears, relaxes all its strain.

BE STILL AND KNOW THAT I AM GOD.

APPENDIX TO CHAPTER 15

IT should be pointed out to beginners that the "quietness" which is spoken of in the foregoing chapter is not a negative passivity, but is the result of a reaching up to God.

To sink down into a negative, passive state is to descend to the astral plane, and this is accompanied by certain dangers. This wrong "quietness" must be avoided at all costs. In prayer and meditation the heart and mind must be lifted up until a point of contact with the Divine is reached. and then the "quietness" should be practised. This is being still and knowing God. The negative form, on the other hand, is being still and contacting Hades.

The stillness of the Inner Presence is not stagnation, but is the stillness of unimpeded activity. Example, a wheel, when revolved rapidly, appears to be motionless.

Chapter 16

THE WAY OF LIFE I

WHAT is Our Lord's teaching, or what is the message that He bears to men? Our Lord came not only to reveal God to us as Love, but also to tell us of the Kingdom and to help us find it and enter into it. The Kingdom! What is this Kingdom of God or Heaven? Is it the discovery of inward powers, as our New Thought friends teach or infer? No. Is it the attainment to immortality in the flesh? No. Is it some place which can be found by dying? No. Is it immortality and eternal life? No.

The Kingdom is something far greater. It transcends them all, even eternal life. The Kingdom of God is so great it cannot be described at all, and the more we try to do so, the more inadequate our words become. Yet we must endeavour to say something about it, in the hope that it may direct our readers' thoughts into the Way of Life, wherein they will have revealed to them, by the Spirit, the great secret of the ages.

The Kingdom of God or Heaven is Divine Union, nothing less. How can we speak about anything so sacred, so wonderful, so sublime, except with bated breath? It is true, although so impossibly wonderful. Nothing less than at-one-ment with God, mystically spoken of as being sons of God, joint heirs with Jesus Christ.

So our ever blessed Lord, who belonged to this Kingdom, and Who forever was and is its glorious King, came to seek and to save them that were and are lost. He came to conduct us into His own Kingdom of union with God. Our

Lord is still with us to help and sustain by His Spirit. He is transcendent in Heaven, yet He is immanent with us. Bless His name.

The Kingdom of God is the Kingdom of the Spirit. It is entirely different from the Kingdom of the World. The Temporal Kingdom can never be the Spiritual Kingdom. Because of this the beloved John wrote: "Love not the world, neither the things that are in the world. If any man love the world the love of the Father is not in him. For all that is in the world, the lust of the flesh, and the lust of the eyes, and the pride of life, is not of the Father, but is of the world. And the world passeth away and the lust thereof: but he that doeth the will of God abideth forever."

The Kingdom of the Spirit can be entered only by those who are lovers of the Spirit. In the Spirit we are all lovers, all brothers, lovers of God, of one another, of our fellow men, even though they be our persecutors and slanderers. In the Spirit
we all speak the same language, although outwardly we may differ as the poles as regards religious belief or doctrine. In the Spirit we are all one.

How precious and wonderful is our Lord's teaching; how rich the treasure that He has to offer. It is the pearl of great price, the hidden treasure, the lost piece of silver. Those who are in search of it give up everything in order that they may acquire this great treasure of Heaven. They leave what they are doing—their ambitions, the baubles of life, worldly fame and glory, in order to search diligently until they find that which is precious above rubies.

How then can the Kingdom of Heaven be found? Simply by following the teaching of our blessed Lord. Like the prodigal son we get disgusted with the husks of the life of the world and the senses. Pleasures become as ashes: sensation brings only satiation and regret. Then, like the prodigal, we arise to go to our Father, to confess our own unworthiness. "Father, I have sinned and am no more worthy to be called Thy son," is the burden of our cry. And when we are yet a great way off, our Father meets us, forgives us and admits us to His own house.

But it is a long journey back. We can be admitted only when we have become entirely at-one with the Father's Will. "Not everyone," said Jesus, "which saith unto me Lord, Lord, shall enter into the Kingdom of Heaven, but he that doeth the Will of My Father which is in Heaven." Neither will belief in dogma or doctrine obtain us entrance, for, said our Lord, "Whosoever heareth these saying of mine and doeth them, I will liken him unto a wise man, which built his house upon a rock: and the rains descended, and the floods came, and the wind blew, and beat upon that house; and it fell not: for it was founded upon a rock." (Matt. 7: 24, 25.)

Chapter 17

THE WAY OF LIFE II

IN order to find the Kingdom we have to put into practice our Lord's teaching, and to follow Him all the way. "Not easy," you say? No, but blessed beyond description. Think of it! The Lord of Life says: "Come unto me all ye that labour and are heavy laden, and I will give you rest. Take my yoke upon you and learn of me; for I am meek and lowly in heart: and ye shall find rest unto your souls." Our blessed Lord, King of High Heaven and all the earth, gives us this loving invitation, and we say: "It is very difficult." And so it is from a human standpoint, but not if we are "swallowed up of love." "For my yoke is easy," says our Lord, "and my burden is light."

In order to find the Kingdom we have to forsake all and follow our Lord. We still continue in the world, but we are not of it. This is a spiritual and mystic separation. It does not mean that we are to sell up and give the proceeds away and live in a monastery, but rather to be different entirely within, loving only the things of the Spirit, instead of those of the world and the flesh. Yet we have to be willing literally to give up all, and even to suffer the death of martyrdom, if called upon to do so. We become non-attached to "things" and "personalities" and at-one with the Spirit. This does not mean that we cease to love, but rather that our love becomes more unselfish, impersonal and universal. The sun of our love has to shine upon both the evil and the good, therefore out Lord says concerning this: "Be ye perfect even as your Father in Heaven is perfect".

And the whole of our life has to be dictated by love. We have to love all, even our enemies and slanderers. We have to forgive freely those who try to injure us and hurt us. It is only as we forgive others that we enter into forgiveness ourselves.

"For if ye forgive men their trespasses, your Heavenly Father will also forgive you. But if ye forgive not men their trespasses, neither will your Father forgive your trespasses." (Matt. 6: 14, 15.)

We have to be the humblest on the earth. We must possess no vain pride, but must take the lowest seat at the table. We must not retaliate when ill-treated, but must be prepared to give up our life, if necessary, for God.

We have to leave off sinning, in word and thought and deed. Our Lord delivers us from all sin, if we only rely entirely upon His Spirit. We have to give up all sin, if we are to enter the Kingdom. Our Lord came to deliver us from sin, and the power of sin, so that we should sin no more.

But all this is only the groundwork, or beginning. We have to follow our Lord into the wilderness to be tempted just the same as He; and because He conquered and was without sin, so also is it possible for us to overcome, in the strength of the Spirit, and through no power of our own.

And this brings us to the kernel of the whole teaching: doing the Will of God our Father, even as our Lord carried out His Father's Will. Because this is one of the stock phrases of organized religion, doing the Will of God may have become nothing but a pious platitude to us, yet in it is the deep secret of all attainment.

What do we mean by doing the Will of God?

God has a most wise plan concerning the life of each one of us. This plan is both wonderful and glorious, and if we will only fall in with it, harmony and peace become ours, and happiness and joy, to an almost unbelievable extent.

We do not have to plan our life. It is already planned for us. This may be a cause of stumbling to beginners, but when we become more advanced we realize that God has a wonderful plan concerning our life, and that the best thing we can do is to fall in with it. Obviously there can be no harmony until we do. Our life is perfect as planned by "our Father." It can become perfect in expression only as we allow God's plan to manifest. We have not to perfect our life: we have only to allow God's perfect plan to be carried out, in every action of our life.

Probably the greatest event in our spiritual experience is when we learn to say with Cardinal Newman: "I was not ever thus, nor prayed that Thou Should'st lead me on; I loved to choose and see my path; but now lead Thou me on."

And again in the first verse:

"Keep Thou my feet; I do not ask to see The distant scene; one step enough for me.'

Chapter 18

THE WAY OF LIFE III

THE Spiritual life is one long series of surrenderings to the Will of God, and non-resistance to so-called evil. Because our life is planned by God, it is therefore good, and all experiences are helps on the way. It is a great day for us when we realize that nothing can come to us that is not good and that all the experiences of life are spiritual, designed by Infinite Wisdom and Love to help us on our heavenly pathway. Because our life is planned by God, and therefore good, it is obvious that we must meet its disciplines, and so-called evil experiences, with non-resistance, with co-operation instead of antagonism.

When apparent evil comes upon us, when unwelcome changes come into our life, of when its foundations seem crumbling beneath our feet, and the dearest earthly props are taken away, then it is that we feel tempted to resist and look upon life and its experiences as evil. But it is not so. It is simply Infinite Wisdom and Love leading us to something that is better.

At such times it is usual to pray God for deliverance. As soon as trouble appears we commence to pray for it to be taken away. That is if we do not know better.

Thus I have known a person to be in Australia, praying frantically to be taken to England; and, at the same time, for a person in England to be praying just as energetically to be taken to Australia. Both were trying their hardest, without knowing it, to increase the disorder of their respective lives. They were both led astray by the

assumption that there was something wrong which
therefore must be put right. They did not know that we are
all led by the Spirit, and that just at the right time we are
taken to the right place where our right work awaits us.
There is no conflict in the Spirit. When the time is ripe and
all things are ready, the way is opened for us, easily,
smoothly and harmoniously; everything falling into its right
place, like well-oiled machinery. All things are always
working together for good.

When apparent evil comes upon us we should say: "What
"good' is it that the Lord is revealing now?" If we do this
we find that all is well and all is love.

While it is helpful for beginners to pray to God for
deliverance, because all forms of prayer are beneficial, and
a more advanced form of prayer is not yet possible to them,
yet for the more advanced seeker there is, obviously only
one type of prayer for him, and that is: "Lead Thou me on,"
or "Father, not my will but Thine be done." God alone
knows the way. God alone can lead us in the right path.
God alone can bring us into perfect harmony and peace.

Yes, this is the only way to the Kingdom; to surrender
completely to the Will of "our Father," to be led entirely
by the Spirit, to give up ourselves and all that we have and
are to God, to live only as Love dictates, to resist not evil,
but to overcome by good. This is the way of joy and peace
and harmony and true content. It is the only path that leads
to the satisfaction of the deep hunger of the soul.

Chapter 19

THE LAW OF SACRIFICE

THERE is a golden thread which runs through all the history of mankind and through all our lives. This golden thread, if followed to the end, leads to the Kingdom of Heaven. This golden thread is the law of sacrifice. It is only through sacrifice that the lower can be raised to the higher. It is only through sacrifice that fallen creation and mankind can be restored to the harmony and perfection foretold so beautifully by Isaiah: "The wolf shall dwell with the lamb, and the leopard shall lie down with the kid; and the calf and the young lion and the fatling together; and a little child shall lead them. And the cow and the bear shall feed; their young ones shall lie down together; and the lion shall eat straw like the ox. And the sucking child shall play on the hole of the asp, and the weaned child shall put his hand on the cockatrice's den. They shall not hurt or destroy in all my holy mountain: for the earth shall be full of the knowledge of the Lord, as the waters cover the sea." (Isaiah 11: 6, 7, 8, 9.)

That which is down cannot raise itself up of itself. It needs help, and this can come only through sacrifice. The lower animals will sacrifice themselves without hesitation in order to save their young from destruction. Human parents give up their all very often for the sake of their children. Those who preach, teach, and write upon spiritual subjects so as really to help others, must develop such a degree of sensitiveness, in order to catch the vibrations of the Spirit, as to make them suffer in a way of which others have no conception. But if they are to help others they must suffer; it is the Law of Sacrifice.

We have to follow our beloved Lord all the way, even to Gethsemane and Calvary.

Each one finds his Gethsemane: each one has to give himself a willing sacrifice for others.

Ah, Yes! The "love so amazing, so divine" that poured out itself on Calvary, and which broke our stubborn wills, winning us for Heaven, must find its echo in our hearts and lives. "Greater love hath no man than this, that a man lay down his life for his friends." (John 15: 13.) All mankind are our brothers, and for them we must willingly give ourselves.

The Way of Life is the Way of the Cross. We must take up our cross and follow our Lord, bearing His reproach. We must take His yoke upon us and learn of Him Who is the meek and lowly in heart, if we are to find rest for our souls.

By self-sacrifice, by crucifying the self, by pouring out our love upon all men, by loving God with our whole heart, mind, soul, and strength, by surrendering to the Will of God, by non-resistance of evil, and by being led entirely by the Spirit, we find our feet firmly planted in the Way of Peace. Then sometimes God in His mercy draws the veil aside so that we enter into that wondrous harmony wherein we seem to rest and recline upon billows or clouds of Eternal Love.

Made in the USA
Las Vegas, NV
19 February 2024